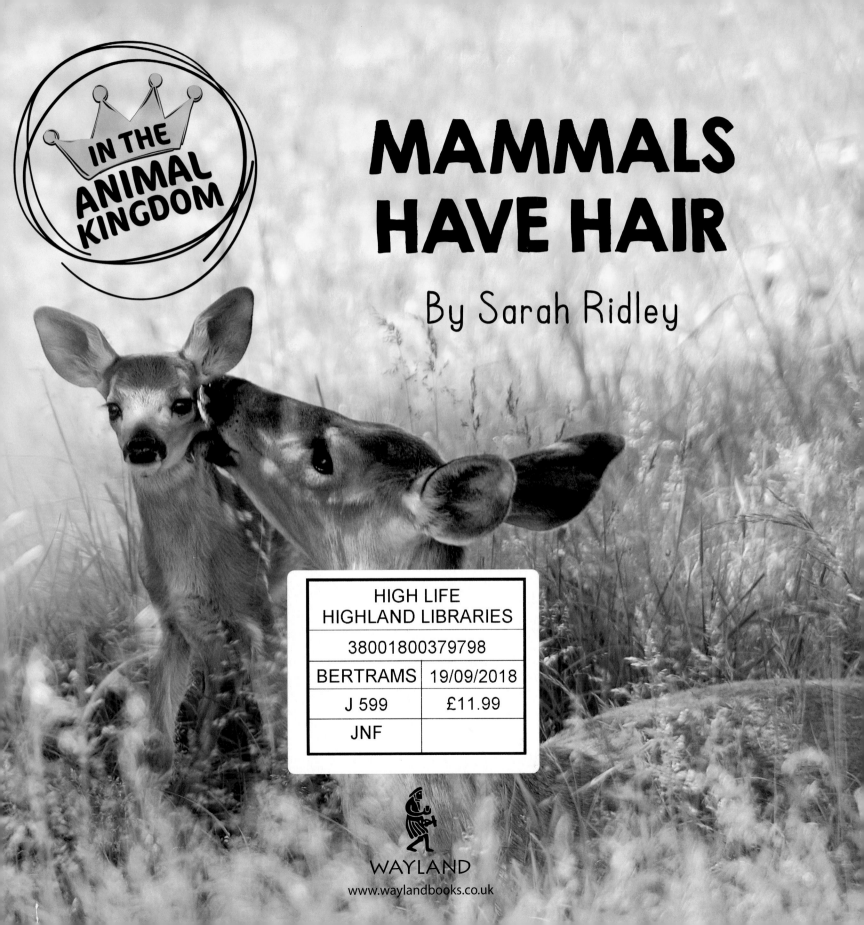

MAMMALS HAVE HAIR

By Sarah Ridley

IN THE ANIMAL KINGDOM

WAYLAND
www.waylandbooks.co.uk

First published in Great Britain in 2018
by Wayland

Editor: Sarah Peutrill
Designer: Lisa Peacock

ISBN: 978 1 5263 0900 6

Printed and bound in China

Wayland, an imprint of
Hachette Children's Group
Part of Hodder and Stoughton
Carmelite House
50 Victoria Embankment
London EC4Y 0DZ
An Hachette UK Company
www.hachette.co.uk
www.hachettechildrens.co.uk

MIX
Paper from
responsible sources
FSC
www.fsc.org   FSC® C104740

Picture credits: AndreAnita/Shutterstock: 6. Eric Baccega/Nature PL:
15t. Neil Bromhall/Nature PL: 7t. Jane Burton/Nature PL: 12.
John Carnemolla/Shutterstock: 18b. GomezDavid/Shutterstock: 10.
Chase Dekker/Shutterstock: 17. Fat Camera/Shutterstock: 7b.
Gary K Gray/Shutterstock: 8. Eugen Haag/Shutterstock: 18t.
Yann Hubert/Shutterstock: 22t. Kertu/Shutterstock: 22bl.
Ivan Kuzmin/Shutterstock: 19t. marianoblanco/Shutterstock: 23b.
pavvia/Shutterstock: 16. Tom Reichner/Shutterstock: 2b, 22br.
M. Rohana/Shutterstock: 13. Andy Sands/Nature PL: 11.
Kim Taylor/Nature PL: 9. Mark Taylor/Nature PL: front cover.
Mary Terriberry/Shutterstock: 1, 14. Taam Voratham/Shutterstock: 2t,
23t. Arend can der Walt/Shutterstock: 3t, 15b. Dave Watts/Nature PL:
20, 21. zaferkizllkaya/Shutterstock: 3b, 19b.

CONTENTS

The animal kingdom

Scientists sort all living things on Earth into five huge groups called kingdoms. All animals belong in the animal kingdom.

The animal kingdom is divided into two very large groups. The invertebrates are animals without a backbone and the vertebrates are animals with a backbone.

INVERTEBRATES

ANIMAL KINGDOM

Then we divide the vertebrates up again, into five large groups: fish, amphibians, reptiles, birds and mammals.

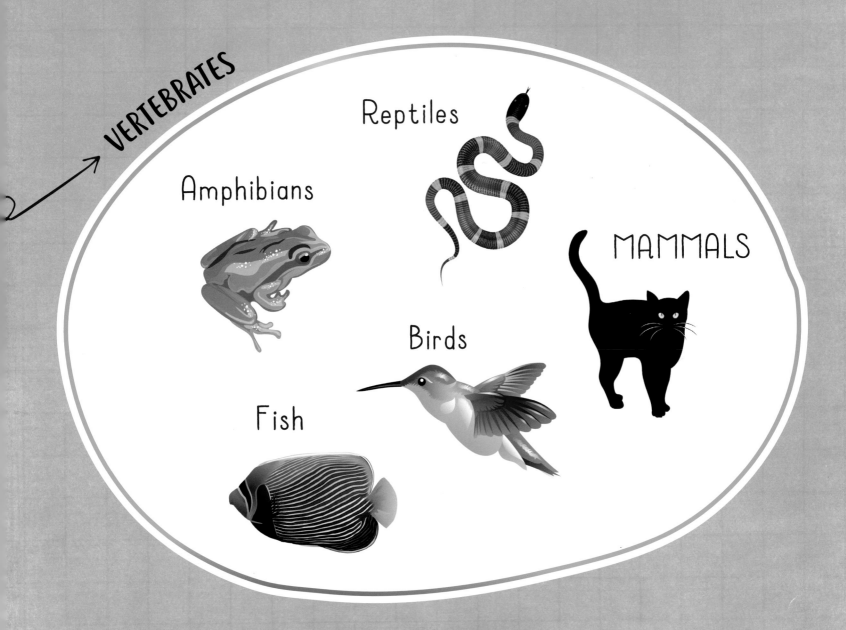

VERTEBRATES

Reptiles

Amphibians

MAMMALS

Birds

Fish

Read on to find out what makes an animal a mammal.
And don't forget — that includes you!

Mammals have hair or fur

All mammals have hairs growing from their skin.

Many mammals have lots of hairs growing close together. This is called fur. Hair and fur help to keep mammals warm.

Polar bear and cubs

Even the naked mole rat has about a hundred hairs on its body.

What keeps your head warm?

Mammals are warm-blooded

Mammals can turn the food they eat into heat – they are warm-blooded. This helps them to keep their bodies at the same temperature, whatever the weather.

Bison

Common dormouse

Some mammals hibernate during winter, when there is less food around. As a dormouse falls into a deep sleep, its body cools and its heart slows down.

Can you name any insects or amphibians that hibernate?

Mammals give birth to live young

A baby elephant grows safely inside its mother for more than a year and a half. Soon after birth it stands up and can walk or run away from danger.

Some baby mammals spend less time growing inside their mother.

This harvest mouse will care for her young for about a month while they grow fur, open their eyes and grow strong.

What are human babies like when they are born?

Mammals drink milk

Four of these kittens are drinking milk from their mother. After she gave birth, her body started to turn the food she ate and the water she drank into milk.

Milk flows out of the teats or nipples on a mother mammal's body. Only mammals make milk to feed their babies.

When you were a little baby, your mother fed you herself or she fed you milk from a bottle.

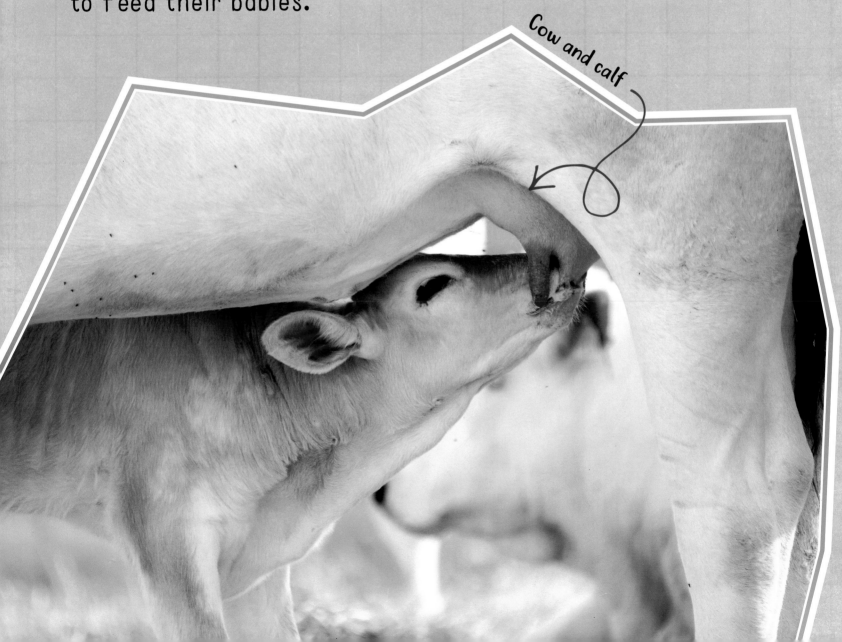

Cow and calf

Mammals care for their young

In the animal kingdom, many animals never meet their parents. However, mammals feed their young, keep them clean and show them how to survive.

Deer and fawn

Grizzly bears teach their cubs to fish.

Young meerkats learn how to keep safe by copying their parents.

What have your parents taught you?

Mammals breathe air

Mammals breathe air using their lungs. In cold weather, you can see your breath when you breathe out.

Take a big breath.
Can you feel your lungs
filling with air?

Dolphins spend their whole lives in water. They have to swim to the surface to breathe air, but can hold their breath under water for a long time!

Soon after it is born, a baby dolphin loses the only hairs on its body.

Mammals move on four legs, two legs or none

Look at these mammals, grazing on grass in Africa. They all move about on four legs and can run very fast.

Kangaroos can hop using their long back legs.

Bats' arms and hands are wings. They hang upside down from their feet when they rest.

Seals have flippers instead of arms and legs.

Some mammals are different

A few mammals are a bit different from the rest. Duck-billed platypuses and echidnas are the only mammals to lay eggs. Once the young hatch, they drink milk made by their mother.

Duck-billed platypus

What else is different about a platypus? And the same?

Marsupials are mammals that give birth to tiny, undeveloped babies. The baby has to work its way up the mother's body and into a pouch, or onto a teat. There it feeds on milk and continues to grow.

Wallaby and its joey

Which animals lay eggs?

Mammals live everywhere

Big or small, furry or almost hairless, mammals live all over the world.

Whales live in the oceans.

Pikas live on cold, high mountains.

Oryx live in boiling hot deserts.

Walruses live in icy places.

Monkeys live in jungles and forests.

People live all over the world, except for Antarctica. These Tuareg children live in the desert in Mali.

Which one of these is the odd one out and is NOT a mammal?

Dolphin   Duck-billed platypus   Penguin   Giraffe

Answer: see below

Glossary

amphibian An animal that can live both on land and in water.

backbone A row of small bones that are connected together to form the spine.

grazing Animals eating grass.

hibernate When an animal slows its body right down so that it can sleep through winter.

insect An animal with six legs and a body divided into three parts.

invertebrate An animal without a backbone, such as a snail, octopus, worm or starfish.

lungs Two organs inside a mammal's body that it uses for breathing.

Tuareg People who live across the Sahara desert in Africa and follow a traditional lifestyle.

warm-blooded Animals that can keep their bodies at the same temperature even when it is cold by changing the food they eat into heat and energy.

young Another word for animal babies.

Answer: Penguin – it is a bird.